Heart and Soul

Poems of Thoughts & Emotions

Mariah Thomas
@realmariahth

ISBN: 978-1724046079

Thank you to my family

& Thank you to my friends

& Most special thanks to the
Woman to whom I came into the world
For her light never fails
To inspire and cultivate
A generation
Of Independent
Minds.

~ *Mariah Thomas*

How the world must have smiled
When you came into *existence*.

And when the name
You were given
Was *spoken to life*

How *joyful* the tears
That fell from the
Sky above.

~ *Mariah Thomas*

Our body is like water
Moving with the tides and swaying with the *wind*.

~ *Mariah Thomas*

My branches have torn
My tree has *withered*
My leaves have fallen
My bark has *rot.*
What was once in full bloom
With a head full of life
Left fetid and *small.*

~ *Mariah Thomas*

Y ou read me like a book

But my words were too *complex* to form coherent thoughts

My spine only *thickened* and my pages were too long

And by the time you finished reading

You never truly understood the *story* I had to tell.

~ *Mariah Thomas*

You told me I was beautiful
But you weren't looking at me.
You told me you loved me
But it wasn't me who you loved.
You loved the mask that was my body
You favored my looks rather than who I was
But when I realized your human desire for physical attraction
I learned that nothing about you attracted me.
I only loved your looks
And I was no different than you who called me *beautiful*.

~ *Mariah Thomas*

You tried to curl your fingers into every part of me
To drag me away from what I held dear
But slowly yet patiently I waited for those fingers to loosen
And with every day that passed a finger uncurled
And I ran to the very place you wished to keep me from.

~ *Mariah Thomas*

I used to think every boy just wanted to have a good time

They just wanted to play with my body then throw me away

Like I was only a tool for their lustful desires

But then I realized that the problem was deeper

I didn't have to let them throw me away

I didn't have to let them into my life

But I did.

And it took me a while to realize

That the ones who wanted to cherish me

Were beside me all along.

~ *Mariah Thomas*

You were my first
But I knew you *wouldn't* be the last
And my heart and body
Surely *never* belonged to you.

~ *Mariah Thomas*

Every tear that fell from my face

Fell upon a *desolate* land

And with every drop grew a blooming rose

And soon a garden of *budding* life.

~ *Mariah Thomas*

My eyes screamed *I love you*
But my lips were too fearful to part
My tongue was too tied to untangle
And my words only ceased to speak the *truth*.

~ *Mariah Thomas*

Bravery is more than jumping in to help others
But having the courage to defend your *body*
Against the inner toxins that wish to contaminate your mind
And damage your *soul*.

~ *Mariah Thomas*

When my daughter matures I want her to know her *worth*

I want her to know that a man's opinion of her

Doesn't determine her *beauty*

I want her to know that the hair on top of her head

Isn't a gateway to instant *attraction*

And that opening her legs isn't a gateway

To social *acceptance.*

I want her to know that her inner *light* shines

With every smile that caresses her face

And that her dreams and aspirations can connect her

With *fruitful* people around the world.

~ *Mariah Thomas*

A woman's shape doesn't define her *sexiness*

And if you believe so

Take her place

To understand the struggle that comes with

Loving one's body and society's physical standards.

~ *Mariah Thomas*

You were simply the bee that wished to deflower my *nectar*
And with the slightest taste, you knew I was *sweet*
Then fluttered away to share what I thought was only *yours*.

~ *Mariah Thomas*

Beyond this world is one that is *limitless*

Where your loved ones rejoice at your return

And your creator smiles upon you

For the *great deeds* you have done.

~ *Mariah Thomas*

I'm more than a *hole* waiting to be penetrated

I'm more than a *release* for another being's pleasure

I am more than a *tool* for a man's lustful desires

And possessive energy

I am more than a *birth giver* and stay at home *mom*

I am more than what society once deemed *weak* for man's work

I am more than the *breasts* that protrude from my chest

I am more than a simple *rib* created from the world's first man

I am more

And I will continue to be more

Despite the barriers that threaten to entrap me.

~ *Mariah Thomas*

Some women choose to follow men
Some women choose to follow their dreams
Both sides have a final destination
But only one will lead to true *satisfaction.*

~ *Mariah Thomas*

There is power in what you speak

My mom tells me

When you speak negative things onto your life

The bad will gravitate toward you

But if you speak positivity onto the world

Not only will your mindset change

Bu you'll begin to see the world in a new light.

~ *Mariah Thomas*

#*Blackgirlmagic* is more than the color of my skin

And the curls in my hair

And my *voluptuous* lips.

But the power in my movements

And the *strength* of my heart

And the *weight* that I carry

On the shoulders that man once deemed unworthy

And the power to prevail and love

The future generations that only

I can bare.

~ *Mariah Thomas*

I'm more than the *color of my skin*

And if you don't think so

Stray away from the path we both take

While I flourish down a road of *endless wonders.*

~ *Mariah Thomas*

The higher my afro grows
The more strength I gain
With every inch and every coil
My *spirit* continues to grow
And my power becomes *immense.*

~ *Mariah Thomas*

Like a *budding* rose

My body continues to grow

It continues to flourish and sprout on any given day

Into a beautiful *floweret* worthy to be plucked

Until one day I will wither

And the petals of my life will forever be engraved into

The soil for continuous years.

~ *Mariah Thomas*

My great grandmother called me her *little princess*

So, I always wore my hair in a braided crown.

~ *Mariah Thomas*

They tell you to open your legs
That it's your duty to let them in
Don't let them take away your shine
Don't let your worth be determined by lust

You are love
Your body a temple for the *creation of life*.

~ *Mariah Thomas*

Why do they hate me?
Because your skin is deep
Why do they taunt me?
Because your hair stands tall
Why do I run?
Because they can't handle God's masterpiece that is you.

~ *Mariah Thomas*

I didn't want to look you in the eyes

Because I could see the *world* in them

You would hold me and I would look away.

But now I truly came to love your tender heart

And accepted that I was your world

As you were *mine.*

~ *Mariah Thomas*

You ever wonder what it would be like to be the wind?
You could turn the tides and sleep on the ocean breeze
You could flow in the distance and watch everything
As it happens
You could *feel* and just be in a peaceful mindset
And when your emotions overtake you
You could blow them all away
And just be *free*.

~ *Mariah Thomas*

I'm not *black* because of the color of my skin

I'm not *black* because my hair defies gravity

I'm *black* because of my history

I'm *black* because of my ancestor's pain

I'm *black* because my culture was taken away

I'm *black* because that's the name you chose to give me.

~ *Mariah Thomas*

I want to fight back

Against the chains bound to my waist

I want to fight back

Against the shackles that hold me down

I want to fight back

Against the anger that shakes my inner core

I want to fight back

So, in the end I will

And in the end, I will win.

And in the end, I will be **unbound.**

~ *Mariah Thomas*

My hair continues to grow

And blossom like a *cherry tree*

My coils curl and swirl like the greens of an *evergreen tree*

My locs hang long and bend to *crown* atop my head

A *queen* born with a curly top

With hair as soft as the *royal* silk.

~ *Mariah Thomas*

Don't fear what others will say about you
Don't fear what they will think.
Fear is only a *shadow*
And they only show spite when they want fear
To hinder your *success.*

~ *Mariah Thomas*

Sometimes I just want to lay

I don't want to go out

I don't want to interact

I don't want to do anything.

I only want to sleep

Think

And eat.

~ *Mariah Thomas*

Sometimes your future is clouded by the past
You can't help but think *what could have been*
Instead of *what should happen next*
Look ahead
And the sky will clear and that cloud will disperse.

~ *Mariah Thomas*

If only Jack didn't fall down the hill

Jill might not have *tumbled*

And their *crowns* wouldn't have been so sore.

~ *Mariah Thomas*

They think I'll be whole if they fill me inside

But they're wrong

Only I can *make* myself whole.

Only I can *fill* what's missing.

~ *Mariah Thomas*

Take off your *armor*

And shed your *wall*

Perfection is only a *dream*

And mistakes are meant to be made.

~ *Mariah Thomas*

I shine when the sun glistens behind the clouds

How am I not magical?

~ *Mariah Thomas*

My hair defies gravity

How am I not a myth?

~ *Mariah Thomas*

I have the power to bring life into this world

Bleed very month

And survive through pain worse than death

How am I not spiritually immortal?

~ *Mariah Thomas*

A thousand heartbreaks should never bring you down

Because with every heartbreak

The closer you are to finding the *perfect* one.

~ *Mariah Thomas*

I can't breathe

Why won't they stop?

I can't breathe

Why won't they let go?

I can't breathe

They finally heard my voice

I can't breathe

But it was already too late.

~ *Mariah Thomas*

They tell me I won't amount to anything

They tell me my work is meaningless

But it means something to me

So, I call it

Poetry

Because

That's what poetry is

A piece of me

A Work of Art.

~ *Mariah Thomas*

Your vibe intertwined with mine
Our hearts beat to the same rhythm
Our souls refused to part
And this outer shell and physical *flare*
Only added to the *lustful* ribbon
That pulled us *together*.

~ *Mariah Thomas*

*E*xotic is a word

I have come to hate.

Exotic is a word

That does not define me

Because it separates me from the norm.

I am truly unique in my looks and my style

Yet my race should not be deemed exotic

Because your eyes have not yet seen

How *normal* the world is

With its variety of looks.

~ *Mariah Thomas*

Every morning I think of my life

And the life of past generations

And I cry

I cry for my ancestors

I cry for their pain

But most of all I cry for *myself*

Because the past is only a piece of me

And I can't seem to forget our *suffering*.

~ *Mariah Thomas*

Go back to your country

Go back to yours.

You don't belong here

Well neither do you.

Besides race is only an *illusion*

And we're all 99.9 percent the *same.*

~ *Mariah Thomas*

When a woman calls me pretty

I only shy away

I shyly accept the compliment

But it doesn't settle

Words shouldn't settle

Because what they perceive to be pretty

I don't.

And only my perception of myself matters

And until my perception changes

Nothing about me will change.

~ *Mariah Thomas*

Our *bodies* stood tall
Our *afros* were thick
Our *braids* grew long
Our bodies were thick.

Our *lips* were luscious
Our *kingdom* grew high
Our *gold* was rich
Our *mind* was wide.

Our *life* was long
Our *crowns* had shined
Our *skin* had glowed
Our *crops* had thrived.

Our *past* was prosperous
Our *land* was blessed.
Tis was a time before the *sins of labor*.

~ *Mariah Thomas*

Life is like a *balloon*

Once it *pops* it can never be re-blown

And the pieces are left to sway to the ground

For another to pick up.

~ *Mariah Thomas*

Why must I be anything
Beyond what your eyes can see?
With hands to touch
And a heart to feel
I am only one example
Of what it means to be *alive*.

I am only one example of
What you could have been
If your life
Paralled to mine.

~ *Mariah Thomas*

I want to be strong
But life just seems to knock you down
Even when you try getting up
You fall even harder.

But isn't that what life is about?
Never losing hope
Endless falls that only make you stronger
And better than you were before.

~ *Mariah Thomas*

If the *wind* howls with the sultry breeze

And the owls hoot in the cool of night

How does the earth feel warmth from the cold

And how does she hide from the *rigid* gust?

~ *Mariah Thomas*

Mama told me not to let them call me names
To love myself and my imperfections
But it's hard.
So hard to look in the mirror and think

What's wrong with me?

What's wrong with them?

~ **Mariah Thomas**

My heart has withered

My blood runs deep

My tears have dried

My mind begins to fleet

Into an endless pool of monologues and thoughts

Acting out what *could have been*

What *would have been*

My life.

~ *Mariah Thomas*

From the day you were born
You were gifted with *miracles*.

Hands to *touch*

A heart to *feel*

A body that *comforts*

And legs that stand above the grassy terrain

And the soil that only yearns to seep into every piece of

What was made

Only for *you*.

~ *Mariah Thomas*

I am *everlasting*

I will forever *glow*

I am a beautiful creation

Of love and peace and tranquility.

My eyes are like *stars*

My lips only speak *life*

My hair is a *crown* atop my head

My body- a blessing upon this life.

~ *Mariah Thomas*

Every time you pluck my feather

I cry a little inside.

Every time you try to piece me back together

I fall apart even more.

Every time you try to make things right

I'm already too *far* away for you to grasp.

~ *Mariah Thomas*

It is so easy to fall into the

Trap called love.

When you love

They do not love back.

What you love

You can never get.

Why you love

Is a question

Many wonder before

Realizing you never had a reason to begin with

As they fall into a repetitive cyle

Of why they chose to love you

And why you never loved them.

~ *Mariah Thomas*

At night I take a hot shower
And let the water caress my fears.

My thoughts and internal battles
Drift away
And all that's left is

Inner peace & tranquility.

~ *Mariah Thomas*

It wasn't easy falling out of love

You hit me like a *crashing* wave

And my walls came crumbling down

I couldn't *re-build* my security.

I couldn't fill in those broken holes.

Because that crack you left was all it took

For everything to fall apart.

~ *Mariah Thomas*

My mom tells me to *learn to be alone.*

I never enjoyed my own company.

But loneliness taught me a lot about myself

And one of those things was that I didn't enjoy being alone.

~ *Mariah Thomas*

Do you love me?

He said no.

So, I left

And I closed that door and never looked back.

~ *Mariah Thomas*

If I could *fly* I would travel the world
Because in my dreams I *soar* the sky
And what I can do is limitless.

~ *Mariah Thomas*

You say you're the only one
But there are plenty of *fish* in the sea
And you were only the carp that
Accidentally got caught in my *net*.

~ *Mariah Thomas*

I loved the way our bodies moved to the same rhythm
I loved how our steps would parallel
And the sweat that would pool from
The intensity of our movements.

We were one when the music *enraptured* us in its spell.
And I was the woman that spoke those magical words of
Enchantment.

~ *Mariah Thomas*

Why share what is yours
When others don't care to give?
Why give so much
When others refuse to give little?

"It's all in your mindset," *my* mom had said.
Do not worry on *how* much they give
But *why* you choose to give to others.

~ *Mariah Thomas*

Black Women

A diverse and strong group of women.

With dark skin and curly hair

With sexy lips and a curvy waist

That cry tears of *gold*

And speak only words of *delight*.

~ *Mariah Thomas*

Beauty is pain

And every time the hairdresser would burn my hair

From the flat iron's heat

I would cry.

I would cry because I wanted straight hair

But now I cry because I once considered straight hair to be

The only way

They'd call me

Beautiful.

~ *Mariah Thomas*

My heart tells me to hate the world
To hate the people who hate me
To hurt the ones who've hurt me the most

Nothing will change
My mind would whisper softly in my ear
Caressing my deepest wants and desires of frustration

Nothing will change
So, I don't take revenge against them.
Because I know revenge won't change a thing.

~ *Mariah Thomas*

Exfoliate your body

Shed your skin of built up contamination

And the world's rotten external core.

Massage every crevice and tightened muscles

Of life's labor

All the while refreshing your outer spirit to undergo the

Continuous cycle of

Enhancement.

~ *Mariah Thomas*

My heart burns like a raging fire

Wishing to be put out

By the only one willing to calm its *aching* flames.

~ *Mariah Thomas*

Stop exploring one's body with Netflix and Chill

And explore the *world*.

~ *Mariah Thomas*

I want to create a masterpiece

A masterpiece only meant for you

With colors that *dance* across the canvas

And emotions that *spill* from my heart to yours.

~ *Mariah Thomas*

Black man walking

Lock your door

Black man walking

Don't let them in

Black man walking

Media says to be afraid

Black man walking

But he's only a child

Black man walking

Is it because he's wearing a hoodie?

Black man walking

He wasn't doing anything wrong

Black man walking

But he was.

He was walking

While

Black.

~ *Mariah Thomas*

I only ever feel at peace

When I distance myself from the outside world

When I indulge in the beauty of my own thoughts

And let my feet soak into the earth from which I came

Placing my hands on the bark of a tree

And letting nature replenish

The body to which has aged

With the passing of man's connection to

Mother Earth.

~ *Mariah Thomas*

Don't let life control you
Because you're the one doing the work
And life is just the *ride* you have to take.

~ *Mariah Thomas*

Possessiveness isn't *love.*

Anger isn't *lust.*

So, don't intertwine the two.

~ *Mariah Thomas*

M y life is flickered with *specks of gold* and

Loving thoughts

Of

Self- admiration

And *fondness* for

Everything that has to do

With being

Me.

~ *Mariah Thomas*

I'm not a figment of one's *imagination*

Or a *shadow* to be kept in the dark

I am not the **darker** sister

Or **darker** mistress

You fondle with in your nightly desires.

I am not the tool

You wanted to make use of

Then throw me away

As you live a life of luxury.

I am like **you**

I am one of you

I am you

But one whose past is shrouded

In the mist of

The human's desire

For

A divided race.

~ *Mariah Thomas*

Don't ever fret

Don't ever fear

Pain is only an emotion.

Life is only an *emotion*.

~ *Mariah Thomas*

I look at the girl in the mirror

And smile

For her eyes hold that youthful glow

That can never be unlit.

~ *Mariah Thomas*

Between us is the cigarette of life.

Life for us because we think it's a cure

But death to others

Because the *smoke*

Doesn't cure their sorrows.

~ *Mariah Thomas*

I close my eyes
Because I want to feel more than your touch
I want to *feel* what you feel
And the love that comes with it.

~ *Mariah Thomas*

My skin is the color of the soil boiling beneath your feet

Lifting the ground from its surface

And *nurturing* the flowers that

Wish to bloom.

~ *Mariah Thomas*

My hands tell the story of a privileged life
A life that differs from my grandmother's
Whose hands have only ached.
A life I had never seen
But one she had known

Where hate filled the world
And forced us to drop to our *knees*.

~ *Mariah Thomas*

*S*ugar

Spice

And everything nice

Are ingredients .

That did *not* create

Me.

~ *Mariah Thomas*

I am made of water
Water without a taste
But a hint of *lemon*
And a pinch of

Salt.

~ *Mariah Thomas*

Hold your breath

Or else you'll *drown*.

Drown from all the emotions

That the tide pulls in

From the back of your

Mind.

~ *Mariah Thomas*

You don't own me.

Your words do not penetrate my defenses
Your hands do not hold me against my will
Your eyes do not capture my inner self

But I own you.
Because my words must have enticed you
To the point
Where you *wished*
I was
Yours.

~ *Mariah Thomas*

When a baby cries

You cry with them

Because they do not

Understand the pain

That comes

With raising

A *piece of you.*

~ *Mariah Thomas*

When I wake in the morning
I whisper prayers of *thanks*
Thank you for a new day.

Thank you
For who
I will become.

~ *Mariah Thomas*

Every morning I look in the mirror and tell myself

I am beautiful

I look at my eyes and I whisper

I am beautiful

I look at my lips and whisper

I am beautiful

I look at my body and whisper that

Everything about me

Is *beautiful.*

~ *Mariah Thomas*

*Y*es
My eyebrows are not the same
They are sisters
And nothing else about me
Is identical.

~ *Mariah Thomas*

I open my arms to embrace
All that is you
Only hoping for the same
Acceptance
In my time of comfort.

~ *Mariah Thomas*

They speak words of hate
But my words will only speak life.
Because the only way to combat hate
Is the sister
Who uses her words of

Love.

~ *Mariah Thomas*

As my pockets grow heavy

And my wallet thickens

So will my love for the people who believed in me

And the ones who dared to

Say my dreams

Would *never* come to life.

~ *Mariah Thomas*

You trickled into my heart
With a thread made of *gold*
That intertwined us together
And glistened like the rays of

A *sun-kissed* bloom.

~ *Mariah Thomas*

My body was a raging fire
Your heart was a withered storm
Together we were unstoppable
But apart

We were only a dull *flame.*

~ *Mariah Thomas*

You can tie your knot around my neck
But my words will not stay silent.

I will continue to *empower*
And *embrace* my roots
Because without it I am nothing.

And nothing is what you want me to be
So I will continue to love

Being Black.

~ *Mariah Thomas*

Stare but do not touch
See but do not feel
I am not an oddity to be *adored*
Or a pedestal to be *uplifted*
But a simple rose
With petals clinging to the stem
From which you had *plucked*.

~ *Mariah Thomas*

Our bodies are so fragile

And so easy to break.

But

So hard

To fix

And put back *together*.

~ *Mariah Thomas*

Why is it my fault?

That your eyes fall upon me when I enter the room.

Why is it my fault?

That your hands are too eager to touch what *doesn't* belong

To you.

Why is it my fault?

That you yearn

For something to the point that you

Try to

Take it.

~ *Mariah Thomas*

It isn't my fault

It's yours.

And no matter how much my

Appearance lures you in

It isn't

And *never* will be

An invitation

For you to

Enter.

~ *Mariah Thomas*

I watched as the birds huddled together in their nest
As their mother wrapped her feathers to cover their *small*

And *fragile*

Frames

As their eyes closed and mouths chirped with relief

Knowing they were in the care

Of a wise and motherly essence.

~ *Mariah Thomas*

To believe in your purpose
Is to believe in your speech
And the words that flow from
The very depths of
Your inner self
And *unspoken* reflections.

~ *Mariah Thomas*

When you have a dream
Be wary of who you tell
For the ones you trust the most
Can hold a wicked flame
That swells in the pits of their
Envious hearts.

~ *Mariah Thomas*

The stories you tell
Are too tempting to trust
And the hands that held on to mine
Were too *rough* for a man
Claiming to be ready

For *release.*

~ *Mariah Thomas*

Am I that *pillow?*

You wish to hold dear

As you soak your wet tears upon my face

And the dread that pours onto my loving heart

Flows from yours to mine

As if I am the *wings*

That are meant to keep you afloat.

I am not that pillow.

I am not your wings.

And I am far beyond being the system

That keeps you afloat

As I slowly loose my own ability to

Fly.

~ *Mariah Thomas*

I let go

Of those rotten leaves that withered and fell to the depths

Below

I let go

As the wind swept across my bending limbs

Patient with me

As I tried to catch the pieces of my lingering past

That I knew could never return to where they had grown.

So, I let go of the old

And shed my bark of the rotting wood

Waiting as *patient as the wind*

For the new to grow in their place.

~ *Mariah Thomas*

Sometimes I do not speak

Letting my eyes wander the room

And the people whose voices

Overpower the other

As if the noise

Staining their ears

Will undo their inability to

Stay silent.

I bide my time

And one by one they turn to stare at my

Silent figure

Eager to hear the words that'll flow from my lips.

For I did not say a word during their discourse

And instead had chosen

To listen.

~ *Mariah Thomas*

I do not chase
What doesn't wish to be found.
Instead I attract
The people I want into my life
Letting the wind carry my dreams
My future and spiraling thoughts
Into the very core of where
This world first took
It's very breath.

~ *Mariah Thomas*

This love that I feel for you

Has been engraved into my past.

This deep craving of self- love

I hoped you bring

Never lasted.

And when the strings that held us together

Ripped apart

At first, I felt nothing

Letting my body cave into the hole

That I dug before you entered my life.

Somehow the hole never refilled

And as many times I tried to bury myself inside

I only climbed high above the dampened earth

Reaching toward the glint of sun

No longer wanting to be buried

Forever.

~ *Mariah Thomas*

You encompass me in your arms

Yet I no longer feel warm.

This must be what it means to fall out of love

And to

No longer be

Enamored with you.

~ *Mariah Thomas*

It's such a worry
Having to stress about
How to fit into society
How my looks will be perceived by the
Glaring eyes of the figures
Too simple to see beyond their
Shrinking gaze.

~ *Mariah Thomas*

When I trim my hair
I can't help but think of how
Horrible it must feel
To be malnourished
And neglected.

And how with every strand that I cut
How *different* it would be
If I only knew how to revive the pieces
That only yearned for my care
And *attention*.

~ *Mariah Thomas*

Soaking my body in the heat of a bath
Is when I feel most *vulnerable.*

The water reverts my straightened tresses
Into the curly mane that refuses to unwind

Like a spreading fire that consumes
The shape of my oval face

As my body relaxes into a pool
Of endless satisfaction
For seeing myself in my
Purest form.

~ *Mariah Thomas*

You are *more* than what
The world sees in you.

You are *more* than the skin
That ages with the passing of time.

You are *more* than the greys
That trickle their way to the top
Overpowering the youth of a color
That continues to fade since the day
You had first seen the light.

You are *more* than what man wants you to be
And the simplicity of their thoughts
Should never tame that budding want
For *growth*.

Mariah Thomas

Made in the USA
Columbia, SC
10 December 2019

84641871R00074